PRAIS_ . . _ . _ _ _ . _ .

First Prize Winner - inspirational category!
20th annual *Writer's Digest* Book Awards
2013 CIPA EVVY Award
2013 Nautilus Silver Award

Writer's Digest Judge's Commentary

The book is well designed, well written, and really stood out from all the other entries in the spiritual category. While most focus on Christianity, Ms. Eckl is all-inclusive and subtle. She gently guides her readers through their grief, by offering up her own experience and insights from her healing process.

It's a lovely book that will both nurture and inspire those experiencing the loss of a loved one, but it would also appeal to anyone, as everyone knows someone experiencing grief. The author is to be commended for her spare eloquence. She makes it seem easy, but it is the selection of details, the zen-like approach, and the completion of thoughts that makes this book a standout.

It's an ideal format in that someone can pick it up and read one or two chapters relevant to their own process and go back again and again for reinforcement or to find sections that relate to where they are in the process. I'd definitely give this to anyone I knew who was in a period of grief.

A Beautiful
GRIEF

Books by Cheryl Lafferty Eckl

Personal Growth & Transformation

A Beautiful Death:
Keeping the Promise of Love

A Beautiful Grief:
Reflections on Letting Go

The LIGHT Process:
Living on the Razor's Edge of Change

Wise Inner Counselor Books
Reflections on Being Your True Self in Any Situation
Reflections on Doing Your Great Work in Any Occupation
Reflections on Ineffable Love: from loss through grief to joy

Poetry for Inspiration & Beauty

Poetics of Soul & Fire

Bridge to the Otherworld

Idylls from the Garden of Spiritual Delights & Healing

Sparks of Celtic Mystery:
soul poems from Éire

A Beautiful Joy: Reunion with the Beloved
Through Transfiguring Love

Twin Flames Romance Novel

The Weaving:
A Novel of Twin Flames Through Time

Twin Flames of Éire Trilogy
The Ancients and The Call
The Water and The Flame
The Mystics and The Mystery

A *Beautiful* GRIEF

reflections on LETTING GO

CHERYL LAFFERTY ECKL

FLYING CRANE PRESS

Published by Flying Crane Press, Livingston, MT 59047
Cheryl@CherylEckl.com | www.CherylEckl.com

Excerpts from "Sweet Darkness" and "What to Remember When Waking" by David Whyte in *River Flow: New & Selected Poems 1984-2007*, © Many Rivers Press, Langley, Washington, printed with permission from Many Rivers Press, www.davidwhyte.com.

The information and insights in this book are solely the opinion of the author and should not be considered as a form of therapy, advice, direction, diagnosis, and/or treatment of any kind. This information is not a substitute for medical, psychological, or other professional advice, counseling, or care. All matters pertaining to your individual health should be supervised by a physician or appropriate health-care practitioner. Neither the author nor the publisher assumes any responsibility or liability whatsoever on behalf of any purchaser or reader.

Cover and interior typography by Nita Ybarra
Cover and interior design by James Bennett

Library of Congress Control Number: 2011944725
ISBN: 978-0-9828107-2-9 (paperback)
ISBN: 978-0-9828107-3-6 (e-book)

Printed in the United States of America.

To those who mourn,
for they shall be comforted

CONTENTS

Though nothing can bring back the hour
Of splendour in the grass, of glory in the flower;
We will grieve not, rather find
Strength in what remains behind,
In the primal sympathy
Which having been must ever be,
In the soothing thoughts that spring
Out of human suffering,
In the faith that looks through death,
In years that bring the philosophic mind.

William Wordsworth

THE MUSIC OF
WHAT'S HAPPENING

IN THE FALL OF 2008 my husband, Stephen, died of colon cancer. In the summer of 2009 I went on a pilgrimage to Ireland, searching within the spiritual "thin places" of the Emerald Isle, where the veil between worlds seems to lift, for the lost connection of my soul to that of my beloved.

It was a very difficult, but ultimately rewarding, journey—most especially because in the quaint village of Kildare I had the good fortune to meet Sister Mary Minehan of the Brigidine Sisters.

She welcomes pilgrims of all faiths (or none) from all over the world, sharing a profound wisdom that teaches and heals—and that changed my life forever.

1

Sister Mary was a longtime friend of the Celtic poet-philosopher John O'Donohue, who had passed away in January of 2008. As my fellow travelers and I gathered in the sparely furnished condo living room that serves as welcome center, she reminisced about her friendship with this great soul, calling him uniquely attuned to "the music of what's happening."

What a charming way to speak of living in the "now," I thought at the time. And from that day I determined to tune my own inner ear to this cosmic symphony that might just become the soundtrack of my life if I could listen well enough.

Dramatic loss produces an intricate melody—a theme with variations on joy and sorrow, presence and absence, tears and transformation. The pieces in this little book are bits of that music, recorded in words as I made my way through what became a year of letting go, reflecting on the mystery of grief—a winding tune that ends on a lilting note of future possibility.

I find this conclusion most encouraging. And I hope you will, likewise, discover comfort and peace in these pages. Reflections one through twenty-four unfold as they were written—beginning in the second full year after Stephen's death. But they can be read in any order.

May they inspire you to listen for your own inner healing music of what's happening.

Prelude

IT'S ALL ABOUT
INTEGRATION

MORE THAN ONCE since my husband's death, I have found myself saying, *I know I should let go of these things, but I just can't do it yet.*

I firmly believe there are no "shoulds" in grief— especially with regards to when and how I let go of objects, feelings, and ideas. So, early in the process, I decided that if I wasn't ready to let go of something, I wouldn't beat myself up about it. I'm glad I approached moving on in that way. It has definitely made life easier.

It was odd, really. I let go of some things immediately. I replaced the bedroom furniture I had wanted to get rid of since my parents gave it to us in 1994.

5

I remodeled the upstairs of our townhome because the carpet and bathrooms had been worn out for years. I gave away most of Stephen's clothes—except for the ones I wore for months after his death and a few favorite items that I still love to look at once in a while.

To generalize the process that was, at the time, pretty chaotic and random, I think I was clinging to anything that helped me keep the feeling of Stephen's physicality close to me while getting rid of things that blocked my ability to put one foot in front of the other.

I had to make changes in the house so it felt like my home, not the empty place where Stephen used to live. I had to get rid of most of his clothes to convince myself he wasn't coming back and to claim even something as simple as more closet space.

It was so hard not to want to die when Stephen did. I see now that what I was doing, a little at a time, was affirming a commitment to keep on living. And I was forging that new life by integrating the many lessons

I had learned and continued to learn from my years with him.

Because I believe that life is for learning and growing, my intention has always been to find meaning in my experiences. It's something Stephen and I talked about a lot, especially in his final months. Looking back at the past three years, I can say with conviction that my letting go process has been based on my ability to integrate the past with the present and to look forward to a future, as yet undefined.

It took nearly a year for me to come to terms with the idea that Stephen's essence or his spirit could still be active in my life. Until I reconnected with him while on pilgrimage in Ireland, I was in a push-pull relationship with the Other Side—sometimes feeling him present with me and other times feeling only the heart-stopping emptiness of his absence.

Once I felt that we had settled into a new relationship with him on one side of the veil between worlds and me on the other, I was able to seriously begin integrating with more of the practical and spiritual lessons he had tried to teach me when he was alive.

Stephen was ahead of me on the spiritual path and there were concepts I simply could not grasp until I had plumbed the depths of my grief and worked through writing our story so that other people could understand our experience.

As I told that story to others, I began to explain it to myself so that now, three years after losing my darling, I feel that I have become more of myself and more of him at the same time. And as that integration has unfolded within me, I have found many lesser or material things simply falling away because I no longer need the tangible manifestation when the essence had become so much a part of me.

For example, I was surprised when I got the strong feeling that it was time to take off my wedding ring— something I wasn't sure I would ever do.

I felt the continuity of our union, but now at a different level. If I was going to encourage other people to keep growing, I had to do the same. I had to admit that I am no longer married. My husband is dead.

Here is what I have learned so far about letting go: If my intention is personal growth and healing, I can have confidence in the inner wisdom of my path to prompt me when it is time to release something—a feeling, an object, an idea. If my holding on to something is more of a cherishing than a grasping, then I don't feel bad about keeping it.

But if I am clinging out of fear, I must consider what I'm afraid of losing and try to find the essence of that thing in my own being. Once I have claimed that bit of goodness as part of my self, I no longer need the outer representation. It simply falls away.

I am getting better at giving myself a break, practicing self-compassion. Only God knows the time-table of my grieving and my letting go. If I can focus on internalizing the meaning and the tough lessons that life has brought me through losing Stephen, then letting go will take care of itself.

It's the best I can do. It is *all* I can do. And I am allowing it to be enough.

Chapter One

RITE OF PASSAGE

I AM HOME NOW FROM ASPEN where I left Stephen's ashes on one of his favorite mountains.

What a magical experience. It snowed last night in the high country, so this morning the tops of the craggiest peaks were dusted with white. We had a light rain for much of the drive from the resort town of Vail where my friend and I had spent the night, so it was misty as we drove up the narrow canyon to the Maroon Bells-Snowmass Wilderness Area.

The road is sheltered on both sides by aspen trees, and they were brilliant gold in the autumn sun that broke through the clouds by the time we arrived.

Walking alone up the trail, I found the perfect spot for Stephen's final resting place under a fallen tree just a bit off to the side and up a hill. It looked like a sylvan temple. I dug a hole and buried his ashes there, gently folding them into the dirt and leaving the little cremation marker with his name on it in the mixture. Then I covered everything with branches and leaves and grass.

It will all be gone by this time next year. Soon the snows will come and in a few months the spring melt will carry away the ashes, blending them into the crystal lake waters that reflect the bell-shaped mountains rising over fourteen thousand feet in the background.

I cried and said a prayer. Almost immediately I felt a burden lift, and then I thought, *How strange that, here again, I have carried Stephen up the mountain.*

For so long while he was ill I had a recurring vision of us being on a high-country hike—each carrying a full-sized backpack. Every so often we would stop and he would give me part of his burden. Whenever that happened, I would struggle for a few days to adjust to the added weight that was tangible to me, although invisible to anyone else.

Today I carried him again, one last time, up the mountain. And then I laid my burden under a tree. It was an appropriate conclusion.

As my friend and I drove back into town, I heard Stephen in my mind, saying over and over, *Keep moving. Don't get stuck anywhere.* It's as if he's kicking me out of the nest—or some place in which I've become too comfortable.

I'm glad to be home now. I've felt a bit weak in the knees all day—sensing a definite internal shift. It will be interesting to see what happens as the next cycle of my life emerges.

Because grief is not rational. It is primal, random, and frequently overwhelming. Nor is it linear. It unfolds in loops and waves, often catching me unawares and disturbing me in the deepest caverns of mind and heart.

It can feel as if grief will never end and that I will never recover. The fact that others have survived being broken open by loss is little consolation in the midst of the self-fragmentation that grief both causes and reflects.

And yet, it is true. It is possible to heal—at least to eventually find motivation for moving forward. The deep challenge lies in discovering a bit more each day about what works while walking a path that can feel desperately lonely and dark.

I am continually amazed at how the tears come at the oddest of times. And then, like today, a sense of wholeness emerges, quite literally from the ashes of what was.

I'm grateful for those moments of clarity. I have worked hard to come this far. And still the Unknown beckons as mysteries of the grieving heart offer more riches of insight and comfort—if I will hold firmly to the process of life unfolding.

Chapter Two

A CONSTANT DANCE

A COUPLE OF WEEKS AGO I was nearly broadsided by a truck running a red light. There is no way I would have survived the impact on the driver's side of my car. The guy was going at least fifty miles per hour and was completely oblivious to my presence at the intersection.

I honked as he sped in front of me. He glanced over with a glazed look on his face, completely unaware that he might have just committed vehicular homicide, had I not followed my rule of always looking before entering an intersection—even when I have the green light.

My sense that day was that if I had really wanted to follow Stephen over to the Other Side, this was an opportunity. But I didn't. I chose life. So I'm still here to continue experiencing how life and grief work together. Sometimes they make us do odd things.

This week I almost sold my house—the one that Stephen and I poured our love into remodeling. The one that bears the imprint of his meditation. The one he made sure I would have to live in after he was gone. It was a weird choice—but something I felt compelled to do. At least until I got rid of piles of junk and old business files and cleaned all the way from the loft to the basement.

I had a nifty apartment picked out and was gearing up for the move. But at the last minute, I just couldn't do it. Suddenly, the house that had felt more like Stephen's than mine became profoundly *my home*. So, literally one day after the "For Sale" sign went up, it came down.

I feel delightfully at home now. All the spaces work. Stephen's presence is tangibly with me, as it has been for quite a while. But things are different. I'm in *my* life now, not *our* life.

Our life will always be a part of who I am. But his injunction for me to not get stuck anywhere seems to actually mean in consciousness—not literally in a location. I can now see myself living here for a long time. And that's a big relief.

I'm beginning to notice a new aspect of grief. It's a constant dance between claiming the present and letting go of the past. My mother reminded me last night that time is a great healer. But I don't think it's actually time itself that heals. It's what we do with the time.

And the real key for me is in continuing to pay attention to what is arising in the moment and following it—and then not being afraid to abruptly change my mind when I get more information that makes the way clearer.

Grieving has made me a little crazy. Or perhaps I was always this crazy. I'm just giving myself permission to dance with the craziness these days. Because I can tell that the grieving process itself is very wise. And moving with it wisely demands close attention.

Chapter Three

RELEASE AS
A WAY OF LIFE

WE LIVE IN A CULTURE so committed to holding on to cherished people, places, and things that it's no wonder many of us have trouble letting go. But when we are faced with our own death or that of a loved one, release is the theme—and it happens over and over as transition, loss, and grief unfold.

I like the term "release" better than "letting go" because it conveys a sense of energy building up and then rushing out to create something new, whereas "letting go" feels more like dropping something we have been clutching.

Nature can be a wise teacher here because there is

labor getting into this world and labor getting out—and that work entails both build-up and release.

I remember how concentrated Stephen became before his death. He was gathering all of his energy into himself, like a rocket being fueled for lift-off. My friend who is a midwife said it's the same for a woman giving birth. Recalling her own experience, she described summoning all of her strength in readiness for the final push to release her child into the world.

So, our lives are book-ended with arduous labor. In birth, the soul is launched on its new odyssey in time and space. In death, it is propelled into a world of light and love that our minds cannot conceive.

Much has been written about these two seminal events. Yet the question remains: How do we let go when we are not the one in labor? Or—are we ever not the one in labor? If that is true, then considering the concept of release as a way of life may prove useful.

This week, a blog reader asked me how a person

could prepare to let go. Here's what I told her: Bloom where you're planted. Be fully engaged wherever life puts you and practice dealing with small changes as they appear. Then when dramatic loss visits your life, releasing into the next phase of existence will be a habit, not a shock.

This means not poisoning today with what many psychologists call "anticipatory grief"—the thoughts and fears about what is coming. It is so hard to resist the mind's tendency to jump into the future when the certain reality of tomorrow creates real pain today. But there is a way through. It is called living in the "now" where perhaps things are not yet so dire.

The knowledge that we are losing someone precious is very sad. I lived with that sorrow for years. And at the same time, I worked very hard to remind myself that Stephen was still with me.

I remember him commenting several weeks before he quit working that some of his co-workers behaved as if he were already dead. Their emotional disconnection was almost worse than his physical discomfort because it made him feel irrelevant and like a burden to his friends.

We both realized that it is natural to shield ourselves from the pain of future loss. We may actually wish that the other person would hurry up and die so we can avoid the lengthy process of watching him diminish before our eyes.

But the real way through today's suffering about tomorrow's sadness is to be present with the moment we are living—concentrating on today's work from which tomorrow's may emerge. This means honoring and experiencing the feelings that arise. It means discussing what is important, even troubling, to us. It means taking care of ourselves so we have sufficient energy for the labor to come. In other words, it means living life with intention and engagement as it unfolds.

One of Stephen's great lessons to me was to enjoy the process of living, not just the results. It's funny that he had to remind me because that was my experience as a musical comedy actress. Every play, song, and dance has a sequence. The grand finale emerges as a result of executing each step with concentration and heart.

So, the way to let go at the end of life is to live with full presence at every moment up to the final good-bye. Have faith in the universal wisdom of the process. And pay attention to the build-up—whether the experience is one of joy or sorrow. Because, in the end, even the deepest loss can transform into the serene freedom of release—if we don't resist how it changes us.

It's all about moving on to the next phase of being. Our souls understand this concept. Our minds just have to catch up.

Chapter Four

Q & A ABOUT
LETTING GO

HERE ARE SOME EXCERPTS from an extended e-mail conversation that took place on my blog.

I was amazed at how deep into her grief process this young woman wanted to go and how present she allowed herself to be with her own feelings. It was an honor to engage with her in this dialogue over a period of several days. Her key questions and my answers are included here.

Q. How much do you think that caregiving affects someone's letting go process?

A. For me, caregiving became a Zen practice in letting

go of my own psychological attachments and blocks so that I wouldn't interfere with Stephen's process of letting go of his life in the flesh.

Yes, I do think that made it easier for me to release him because I could feel how ready his soul was to take flight. And I think many caregivers would agree that wanting your loved one to be free of suffering makes it easier to let them go and to come to terms with their now being on the Other Side.

If we are open to learning, caregiving teaches selflessness in a way that, to my mind, no other experience can do. I was so aware of needing to be fully present for Stephen while staying out of his way.

This practice of being present for him translated directly into my being present with my grief when that part of the journey began. It was like practicing for the long haul that survivors face. I know my grief experience has been much richer because of being so engaged with Stephen's passing.

Q. Does the very choice to caregive change your connection to someone you love in some sort of a mysterious, visceral way, so that by definition you experience grief differently?

A. What's particularly difficult about giving care is that it can really change the relationship. Children assume more of an adult role with their parents, who may become increasingly child-like. And spouses find it hard to remain lovers and friends when nurse-patient seems to predominate.

This is one reason I so value the role of palliative care and hospice during a progressive or terminal illness. The professional caregivers assume a great deal of the medical burden and they help define the personal dynamics so that family members and spouses can retain more of the original relationship.

Of course, it does change as our loved one slips away, but we are able to remain more familial and less clinical at the end. That is a great blessing.

Q. What does it do to you, when you choose to insert yourself into someone's death process by way of tender selflessness?

A. My sense of caregiving is that we do not so much insert ourselves into another's dying process as we are invited into it. Of course, this is under the best of circumstances. But I have great faith in the way the Universe arranges these things. Even if someone feels unjustly selected as caregiver, I suspect that there are deep reasons for the relationship.

Q. What do you do when someone refuses to help with caregiving or even attending the funeral or burial service?

A. This really becomes one more way of letting go— releasing each other from even subtle expectations of what we should or should not do. People sense when they are respected and, in that sense of being released from external pressure, they often choose to engage— where, before, they might not have done so.

Again, a truly generous approach to caregiving is to extend great gentleness to self and others as we go through the process of loss and grief.

There may be an extended group of family members and/or friends involved, but each of us makes this journey in our own way, at our own time. Respecting that is one of the highest expressions of love.

Chapter Five

THE IMPORTANCE OF RANDOM CONNECTIONS

LAST FRIDAY I DID a book signing at Barnes & Noble Booksellers in downtown Denver. It was midday, with lots of people bustling through the store on their lunch hour. Some were on break from a convention. Others were having meetings in the café. I was strategically positioned near a common thoroughfare, so I took the opportunity to talk to people about what "a beautiful death" might mean to them.

I was pleasantly surprised to discover that many actually had a positive reaction to the possibility that life could end beautifully. Not all, of course. But at least some were open to the idea and stayed to chat.

I found myself particularly drawn to people with positive expressions. It also helped when they met my gaze rather than pretending I wasn't standing right in front of them, offering to tell them about my book.

Towards the end of my event, a lovely man walked by and seemed quite open to hearing my story and then letting me sign a book for him to purchase. Little did I know that he had a different intention. Here is the rather surprising e-mail I received from him yesterday.

To: Cheryl
Subject: Thanks for selling me this book the other day

You stopped me, holding out your book for me to hold while you carefully extolled ("extolliated"—new word). The only gracious way to extricate myself was to ask you to sign it. You not only signed it, you got my first name out of me and wrote it to me.

Well, so much for my initial plan. I could no longer leave it in the downstairs of the bookstore and go about my day with peace. Leaving it behind became an act of vandalism unacceptable to me, and the price—change from a twenty—did not set me back any.

The natural reticence about reading it melted away when she who must be obeyed [*I think he means his wife*] thanked me for buying it when she heard the story. So I hunkered down and finished it this morning, less the afterword portions which I am saving while the read percolates.

Coming at the book from having lost my dear, tormented father—he was with the troops that found and liberated Dachau (a grisly, grisly episode)—and having literally lost control of myself while grieving for him, I could not dismiss you as easily as if you had stayed behind the little desk the bookstore had put out for you. I admired your brave move out from behind that little high wall of a desk.

Gaining control of myself after my dad passed involved knitting back together a decade or more of riotous self-indulgence (which in some ways was made more so by his presence through those years), which amazingly my marriage survived. And now my marriage has become the very base and pinnacle as well of my remaining assets.

The presence of death—our culture is swimming in it—has become a sort of gift, as it must if one is to live with joy, gratitude, and humility and compassion. I am actually excited about eventually dying and am in a constant game of imaginary chess moves with those final stages whatever they may be, however short or drawn out, delicious terror.

Thanks for the read. It was delicious.

Chapter Six

FINDING SOUL SPACE

MY HEART IS YEARNING for something really tender right now—almost as if I'm trying to feel my way across the veil of time and space to wherever Stephen is. Or perhaps I'm just trying to find my own soul—wherever it is.

This has happened a lot since Stephen has been gone. But now that it's holiday time, the yearning is more insistent, the need more acute for what I'm calling soul space—that state of consciousness where I feel connected with myself, other people, the spiritual universe, and with my late husband.

As long as I was working on my book, I felt profoundly connected in that very creative space. To write well, I had to sink into my heart and pull out my deepest thoughts and feelings. In working to contact Stephen's spirit and convey that essence through our story, I could only operate from a place of personal authenticity.

Spending hours a day in that deliciously connected space also allowed me to contact a healing source that I can only identify as Spirit. Whenever I could allow myself to really grieve—letting the tears and despair just flow out of me—that feeling of being comforted by something more than my human self would always flow in.

However, since finishing the book, the more that life thrusts me back into the workaday world, the less connected I feel with my soul, with Spirit, and with Stephen—and the more desperate and exhausted I have become.

Unlike most people, who must return to work mere days after losing a loved one, I am just now finding myself up against the conundrum of soul space versus the necessities of daily life.

My grieving heart has a profound desire to go deeply within. To commune with Stephen's spirit. To rest in the ambiguity that dramatic change has thrust upon me. To fully experience both the waves of grief and the waves of healing that flow from the secret recesses of my heart.

But life calls me back to the surface where jobs, family, and financial obligations demand my full attention. The added expectations of the holidays only add to the burden and the sense of isolation and separateness that make grief seem an eternal purgation.

Now that I'm in the thick of try-to-grieve-and-heal-while-you-work, I realize what a luxury it has been to stay home and rest and write rather than returning to the world that grievers with nine-to-five jobs must face. I simply had no idea how hard it is to heal in a culture that does not support the deep grieving process.

So, I see that being gentle with myself now is even more critical than when I could hide out in my home office all day. Soul space doesn't just happen by itself. I must create time for it, making it a priority—as if this purposeful idling will determine how well I move forward in life.

I think it may be exactly that important.

Chapter Seven

PAYING ATTENTION
TO OUR RHYTHMS

As I HAVE OBSERVED and reflected upon the states and stages of my own grieving process, I have come to the conclusion that—at least for now—following the lead of my body is the shortest route back to the soul space where I have felt healing taking place. The key for me is self-care—which I learned much about from my gorgeous, black standard poodle, Bentley.

Bentley was barely fourteen months old when Stephen died. So, like most growing boys (human or canine), he loved to run and play, eat and sleep. If he didn't get enough exercise, he got into trouble. If he was tired, he just flopped down for a comfy snooze. And when he was eating, he just ate—concentrating on each mouthful with admirable focus.

Being a dog, Bentley didn't have to get up when he was tired, eat lunch at his desk, or skip getting outside in the fresh air. At least two or three times a day, he got to experience the natural world of pungent smells, sights, sounds, and textures. And he was always getting pets from one of his humans—making him a self-assured, happy, friendly, loving creature who acted primarily from a standpoint of, *What do I want to do right now?*

Of course, his humans did their best to channel that desire into, *What are my pack leaders asking me to do?* Something Alpha Dog (Stephen) was more successful at accomplishing than Beta Dog (Cheryl).

Bentley's self-care system functioned well until Stephen died. Then our dog pack fell apart. Alpha Dog was gone and I was not doing a good job as his replacement. So Bentley decided it was his job. He tried to be the boss—a role he was woefully unfit to assume.

Being an immature teenage dog, he really wasn't up to the task. You have to give him credit for trying, but what happened to Bentley was that he stopped paying attention to his own rhythms. He lost his center and got out of touch with his doggie soul space.

At the time, all I knew was that I was ruining him. He needed a home with a clear pack hierarchy and a strong alpha dog. With the help of some truly divine intervention, I found him a new family that included two men, a yard, and a mature female boxer who wasn't going to let an adolescent rule.

That was in 2009. I've since heard that Bentley settled down really well. Of course, he did—he got his rhythm back.

———————

So, how does this story of a grieving dog relate to a grieving human being? In several ways:

- Loss disrupts our pack structure, both at home and at work.

- We may rightly or wrongly assume that it is our job to fill in for the person who is gone.
- In trying to take on other people's responsibilities, we may lose our own center.
- We may get out of rhythm with our own essence.
- We don't know what's good for us.
- We block the subtle physical sensations and emotions that could prompt us to better self-care.
- Instead, we may use more work and unhealthy behaviors—such as abusing drugs, alcohol, or medications—that numb our grief rather than helping us to work through it.

Listening to the body is key. In Bentley's case, I also had to observe his behavior and interaction with me. This is something we can do for others and then support them in practicing self-care.

For myself, I have to pay attention to the physical signals my body is sending and to the emotions that are arising—especially if they are negative or troubling in any way. If I act on these subtle warnings that I need to slow down, breathe, stretch, and eat something healthy, life proceeds more naturally. I also seem to suffer less mentally, emotionally, physically, and spiritually.

Bentley would be so proud!

Chapter Eight

FLOWING LIKE WATER

MY ACUPUNCTURIST SAYS that grief is hard on the kidneys because our bodies are eighty percent water, and kidneys deal with the water element—which is also energetically connected with emotions.

Kidneys help balance the yin and yang (feminine and masculine) energies in the body. Too much yin, and we're damp, weepy, and emotionally out of control. Too much yang, and we push too hard, get hot, irritable, and reactive—and we burn out.

This is one reason I'm so tired these days because I processed the first year of my grief by working, working, working. So now it's Chinese medicine to the rescue and plenty of rest so my kidneys can heal before I charge off into the next set of projects.

I wonder if the natural tendency to go into over-drive after dramatic loss could be an unconscious attempt to compensate for the flood of emotional energy in which we flounder. Conversely, in order to heal our grief, I think we have to become one with that water element and allow ourselves to get into its flow.

While Stephen was still alive, *You can't push the river* was our motto. This didn't mean giving up on treatment when there was still hope. But it also didn't mean trying to outsmart the dying process. In the end, the body had to pass away. We were paddling down a mighty river with big boulders in the channel. Our job was to flow around them, not challenge them.

So, how do I get into a healthier, more positive flow without feeling fragmented by my obligations? Perhaps counterintuitively, it is by allowing myself to go where grief would take me.

I am convinced that grief is very wise. Being one of the most watery of emotions, it flows. It is always moving. Sometimes underground. Sometimes on the surface.

But it is always at work, carving new pathways of awareness that can lead into the next phases of life—if I will trust its wisdom. If I will let go of my impossible expectations and accept that grief itself will connect me with my soul in a way that no other emotion can do. Perhaps not even love.

This holiday season I'm committed to giving myself some private time to cry, journal, reflect, meditate. To go deeply within and do nothing for a while. In tears and in the rich nothingness of watery grief, I am hoping to find courage and inspiration for the days to come.

Chapter Nine

TAKING TIME OUT TO CONNECT

I HAVE NOTICED a difference in people who have experienced dramatic loss and who have honored the vagaries of their own grief process. There is a softness about them—a look of compassion in their eyes that says, *I know what suffering is.*

There is a tinge of sadness that sometimes comes out in the voice. And yet, there is a light, a knowing, a sense of hope and faith that shines through because these people have been touched in their souls by the profound part of life that is its ending.

Grief—if we follow its lead—can kindle in us a soul awareness that does not go away, even as we move

A BEAUTIFUL GRIEF

on. People will say, "You never really get over loss"—
which is true. And, why would we want to? Our love for
the ones we have lost will always be a part of us. We are
who we are today because of them.

Of course, we don't want to continue living in
the deep, unhealed pain where many people stay stuck
for years. But for me, that "Stephen-sized hole" in my
personal universe is a rather counterintuitive reminder
that although the body is gone, the spirit remains. And it
is the spiritual connection that ultimately heals. Not just
my spirit connecting with Stephen's, but my soul connecting with the Divine Presence that lives within me.

Stephen knew this so well. Even though he grieved
at the thought of leaving me behind, his strongest intention was soul union with his Divine Source. He believed
in that ultimate reconnection as the only true and final
healing of the sense of separation that lies at the deepest
root of all our grief.

I am finding that in order to contact that same

50

knowing, I have to be very still. Change my priorities. Stop trying to be superwoman. Rest. Cry. Laugh. Play. Find people to connect with by sharing in a genuine and loving way.

This week I took a mental health day. I returned to my journal for the first time in days, which actually felt like a guilty pleasure. My office is still a disaster. Only part of my Christmas decorations are up. I have some shopping to finish. But all that will wait. And all the to-dos will go faster when I'm back in my own rhythm because now my body is relaxing. I'm breathing again. I'm back in soul space.

Isn't that what holidays are all about? A "time out" to reconnect to that authentic part of self that is always one with Spirit. It's a state of being we can practice visiting in stillness until soul space becomes a familiar place where we heal a bit more each day.

Today a new friend asked me to sum up the focus of my book. That question always stumps me with too many possibilities. For example, it's the story of how Stephen and I lived and loved and lost each other and then found a spiritual reconnection that carries many deeply personal meanings for me.

The story also offers a variety of meanings for other people. But that's not really its essence.

As I fumbled for an answer, my friend cut right to the heart of the matter and said, "I think it's about loving while you have the opportunity."

Isn't that perfect? Make the connections now while you can—with everyone you love. With every thing you love. With life itself. Engage in the moment and see what blessings flow back to you—even if some of them come in the guise of heartache and sorrow.

I've been writing about coping with the holidays and doing radio interviews on the same subject. Today, in the hush that Solstice brings to the December hub-bub, I feel that the key to thriving at this time of year is in making connections. If you are alone, be still and ask yourself what it is that makes you feel connected to life, to Spirit, to your own heart. Then dust off your loneliness and do that very thing.

If you know someone who is alone, invite her to connect. Ask what she would like to join you in doing and do that. Or, it's okay to admit that you don't know what to say to ease his burden. Letting him know you care and that you would like to include him in your holiday celebration can go a long way.

The point is to connect during the holidays and don't stop when the season is over. What would happen if we dedicated ourselves to staying connected in the New Year? Imagine how much kindness and compassion we could generate if we formed that habit.

In order to enjoy more events with people this year, I have given myself permission to not send out Christmas cards. But if I did, I would sign them:

Wishing you time out
for deep connections this holiday season.

Chapter Ten

THE HEALING POWER
OF GRIEF

I THINK THAT grief is made more difficult by a failure to process change and loss throughout one's life. When circumstances deal us a blow or even a mild disappointment, we don't know what to do with the emptiness that follows the shock.

Instead of using it as inspiration to release our sense that *this shouldn't have happened* and venture more deeply within for meaning and resolution, we look for external ways to fill the void.

Years ago, when I lost an election for high school student council president by one vote, my mother took me shopping to make me feel better. It was a kind gesture, but not necessarily the right remedy. I was old enough to learn something about pride and attachment to accolades and power, but I didn't. Instead, those lessons came later and often in more challenging forms.

Perhaps it's the fact that I am still exploring my own grief journey that makes me so acutely aware of it in others. Whatever the cause, that awareness is showing me that there are among us thousands of emotionally wounded people who are stuck in various phases of trauma and sorrow, unable to move forward into acceptance, resolution, and healing.

Over the past few years, I have had occasion to observe this challenge in the experience of some elderly people. A lifetime of churchgoing did not guarantee them a sense of peace, unless, like my father, they were fortunate to also have a rich spiritual life that often developed outside of their regular Sabbath attendance.

My dad had a deep connection with God that he never talked about. He only mentioned it to me a

couple of years before he died after receiving a false positive cancer report. Then we had a long talk about life and
death. I wanted to know that he was okay with God and
he wanted to know that I was happy with Stephen. (Big
thumbs up on both counts.)

In that conversation my father told me about his
boyhood experience of feeling Jesus' presence at a revival
meeting when he went up to answer the altar call. He
said the "warm feeling that everything would be okay"
had never left him. When he did eventually pass away,
I could see that inner peace reflected in the smile that
traced his lips immediately after he died.

A dear lady I know says she has never really experienced that kind of surety. She has a very strong sense of
life's transitions and has made many decisions based on
what felt right as she stood on the threshold of change.

I know she is intuitively connected, but the deep,
soul comfort she has always wanted appears to elude
her. She doesn't seem to have the spiritual confidence

she would like to have in dealing with her current situation. Or perhaps I'm underestimating her.

She is often depressed about her arthritis pain and loss of mobility, and her companion is distraught over his increasing dementia, brought on by a stroke he suffered several years ago. They try to focus on the love they found in each other as widowed persons in their eighties and the good years they have shared, but this gradual loss of the physical self causes a daily grief unlike any they have ever had to bear.

In the face of such protracted suffering, it is hard to find or give comfort. And yet, I have this sense that grief is God's ever-present remedy for our inevitable tribulations of living in time and space.

I am convinced that if we allow ourselves to deeply grieve our losses and explore their inherent lessons, we can receive the blessing of connection that comes from letting the process carry us inward and upward to profound soul work.

It is as if life is destined to break our hearts. But the fact that we have hearts that *can* break is a sign that we are essentially spiritual in nature and, therefore, able to connect with the Divine. The broken heart can actually bridge worlds and enter into a communion with Spirit that is not normally available to a mundane consciousness.

It's a different, higher state of openness and vulnerability. In that moment of knowing that *we can't do this alone*, a divine comforter intervenes.

There is something in our relinquishing the illusion of power in this world that makes it possible for true comfort to be given. In our helplessness, we are given the spiritual strength to move forward and the deeply personal understanding that there is so much more to life than merely what we experience in the body.

I honestly think that realization of our ultimate powerlessness may be all that God needs of us, but we fight it so hard. Or the ego does. That small, rigid sense of self is so stubborn and defensive. It knows that if we admit our vulnerability and start intentionally relying on spiritual communion, it has lost. And that, to me, is actually what life is all about—replacing the smallness of ego with the largeness of Spirit that is always available to us.

Grieving deeply in the moment of losses large and small is one way to get there. In the years following high school I eventually learned to let go of lesser disappointments, petty attachments, and the subtle emptiness I felt when my life changed. That habit of perpetual release has served me well in the face of dramatic loss.

Stephen and I also worked together on letting go during the four and a half years of his illness. As the final parting approached, we were able to use that practice as impetus to reconnect with our own soul space— which is where I have felt healing happen and where life continues to move me forward in love and blessing.

Chapter Eleven

WHY OUR MORTALITY ASTOUNDS US

SOME PEOPLE CLAIM that we are spiritual beings having a material experience. Others say we are material beings trying to have a spiritual experience.

For me, it is the interplay between our divine and material natures that makes being human so fascinating and yet so frustrating. It is also this cosmic dance that explains why our mortality so astonishes us when its reality comes crashing into our lives, disrupting the plans we have made for a rich and enjoyable future.

Ceasing to exist is not a concept we easily entertain. Nor should we. Because in many belief systems the "I" does not cease to exist—it merely changes bodies.

We understand this at deep levels of our psyche. What shocks us is the realization that the time to lay down our present body may be upon us—or upon someone we hold as dear as life itself.

Several months before Stephen died from metastatic colon cancer, he became acutely aware of this dichotomy at work in his being. On the one hand, the divine nature that he strove daily to embody was not afraid to die. In fact, as we read books about the soul's journey from this world to the next, he would weep in recognition of the unspeakable love he felt waiting for him on the Other Side.

To Stephen's soul, departing this life would be a glorious rebirth and reunion with the Divine Presence that he contacted with increasing power and frequency in the meditations that sustained him. There was no fear in this exquisite communion.

And yet, as his strength began to ebb—his physical form weakening from the terrible disease that was consuming it—he became aware of the body's fear of its own impending death.

It seemed remarkable to me that he could sense these two, so very different, forces coexisting within him—and to so clearly differentiate between their processes. But it was not unusual for him to say, "My body is anxious right now," and then become very still.

Losing his body was difficult for Stephen because he had always been so strong and healthy. He had suffered athletic injuries, but never disease. He was accustomed to his body enduring, even growing stronger, under duress. But now it was his soul that had to rise to the challenge of his transition—and rise it did.

In the last few weeks of his life, he etherealized before my eyes, until one day he declared, "There is nothing to fear from here on out." He did experience some agitation and even sudden physical pain in his final days, but I do not believe his body was any longer afraid because of the grace with which he slipped away.

So, coming to terms with the fact that the body must die in order for the soul to move on is a challenge for each of us. Our mortality astonishes us because—even if we doubt the existence of an afterlife—we are more soul-directed than we may realize. It is as if we sense a continuity of consciousness that exists before and after life.

In a way, we play out the drama of death and rebirth every night when we go to sleep and then arise the next morning. And the fact that we do wake up creates a sense that we always will.

So we manufacture elaborate distractions to deny the body's eventual demise. We refuse to discuss death. We invest millions to keep bodies artificially alive, even when souls are ready to move on.

And yet there is a gentle tenderness between body and soul that we can tap into if we allow ourselves to rest in the dichotomy that we are spiritual as well as material beings.

Chapter Twelve

HOW OUR MORTALITY CAN INSPIRE US

I DON'T WAKE UP EASILY. Coming back to my body after sleep has always been a chore for me, as if I'm putting on a garment that doesn't quite fit. Or perhaps I'm not entirely sure I can trust the body to do my bidding throughout the day.

That pattern of distrust was set early for me as a sickly child who was allergic to dust, pollen, animal dander, most foods, and my father's cigarette smoke. Waking up in the morning was to reenter a toxic world that I was powerless to escape.

But these days I have a deeper appreciation for my body—especially for its remarkable ability to enhance my understanding of the thoughts and images that make up my world. Because, after years of listening for spiritual direction, I have come to recognize the body as a brilliant receiving device that unfailingly reflects this moment's truth.

In recent years I have also discovered tears as the surest barometer of that truth. Have you ever been in a lecture or religious service or heard a particular musical passage that moved you to weep? What caused those involuntary tears?

It is as if the body is an instrument on which the soul plays its deepest music of love. We think of intuition as a mental activity—an inner knowing. But, personally, my most profound insights arrive as a gut feeling. Only later can I put words to that sensation—an attempt that often falls short, failing to capture the brilliant *a-ha!* that landed with a perceptible, physical *ka-chunk!* in my belly.

From the perspective of neuroscience, this is the right brain speaking. The left brain is the linear, chatty part, while the right brain doesn't do words. It communicates holistically in physical sensations that sometimes include images and sounds, smells and tastes.

So to ignore these somatic intimations of awareness is to deny intuition, imagination, and the creative spark that puts experience together in the most unique and surprisingly practical ways.

This makes life in the body not only key, but essential, to the interplay between the spiritual and material worlds. Rather than being a tiresome nuisance that gets in the way of our loftiest spiritual aspirations, the body could be considered a critical point of contact between the soul and Spirit.

So, back to those spontaneous tears. What comes first—the tears or the emotions? The sequence is quick, but in many cases the tears are the first to arrive. We may even have to sit with them for a while, following their sensation into a recognizable emotion that we can then think about and describe.

My experience of these instant tears is that—even if the realization is a hard one—they often evoke a sense of truth that comes with a deep sense of joy. To me, this is soul happiness—not only for the liberating power of truth itself, but also because it means that my dense, outer awareness has just experienced a profound communication directly from my soul. And what was the vehicle for this startling bit of awakening? The body.

What a travesty, then, that centuries of religious doctrine have vilified the physical form—encouraging us to negate our ability to tune into that faithful servant's subtle messages of love, illumination, and warning.

Have you ever had a gut feeling that you shouldn't go somewhere or be with a certain person? Perhaps you ignored that gentle suggestion and powered through— only to later discover that you should have paid attention. That's the wise soul and the receptive body trying to protect you.

So, my experience is this: When I am attentive to

my body, my life feels delightfully soul-directed—as if I am in conscious partnership with the Divine.

Like John the Beloved resting his head on the bosom of Jesus, I have the sense of my soul leaning into the heart of God and then telling me what she hears. She speaks into the body and the body forwards the message in a way I can receive—but only if I allow myself to *feel* the communication, wherever and however it lands.

Chapter Thirteen

IN CELEBRATION
OF THE BODY

I HAVE THIS WONDERFUL DVD of short yoga programs
that I love because I will actually do fifteen minutes of
yoga at the beginning of my day. And when I give myself
this time to stretch, the day takes on a lovely, numinous
quality that I totally miss if I just charge into my to-do
list without conscious preparation.

One thing I've noticed is that this yoga instructor
and others I have known frequently use "m-m-m" to
acknowledge when someone else speaks the truth—as if
they are allowing the truth to resonate in their bodies as
well as their minds and hearts. They feel the truth. They
breathe it in and let it nourish them at deep levels.

This behavior may be unconscious on their part, but I believe it happens naturally when a person has developed the habit of body awareness.

It is so much easier to go within when the body has stretched and is centered. The body's health really does become a metaphor for total well-being. It internalizes and mirrors our wholeness or lack of it. The body out-pictures the interconnectedness of all things. It reflects our level of self-care and may even demonstrate our consciousness in action.

Of course, this does not mean that people who are spiritually and psychologically whole don't get sick. We know that they do. We live in a world that is beset with illness, and even the best of us have physical vulner-abilities. But we can influence many aspects of our wholeness—if we pay attention to the subtle messages and reflections our body offers.

Abraham Lincoln reportedly said that, after the age of forty, every person is responsible for the appearance of his or her face. What he meant was that the face is a mirror of consciousness. And the eyes are not only windows to the soul, they can also reflect the extent to which the soul is present and active in the person.

Is there a spark or dullness in the eye? Does the face light up with the fire of spiritual connection? Or is the expression morose, angry, or even crazed?

The body also projects personality. One thing I learned early in my acting training was that by holding a certain posture or expression, I could do more than merely portray a character's personality and intent, I could actually enter into it—literally becoming that person.

Stepping out of that character at the end of a performance was very important, lest my own identity become little more than a collection of assumed personalities. I had to remove the psychological costumes and don authentic garments of my own consciousness if I was going to come back to myself.

Here is where the interplay of body, mind, and spirit comes to the fore. Just as I learned to act as if I were the character, I have also learned to hold myself in an aligned posture that may not yet be reflected in my consciousness.

This is one reason that a body practice such as yoga is so powerful. The only way to hold the yoga positions correctly is to be balanced and aligned with an inner plumb line of the body's original design. Eventually, the practice can become habitual, and that is a good thing.

I think it is true that "our issues are in our tissues." If we practice moving and holding our bodies in healthy physical postures, we can eventually release erroneous patterns of thought and feeling that have contributed to an out-of-alignment state.

As our consciousness becomes more elastic, our body will follow suit. It remains true that my body is only as flexible as my current state of consciousness. There is no such thing as a balanced, crabby shoulder stand.

So, I try to feel truth with my entire being—embracing wholeness with arms extended in welcome. Stretching up to the light, allowing it to shower me with blessing and radiance, I am still amazed when healthier patterns appear. It is as if the stretching gives rise to an increase of spiritual fire in my being.

"M-m-m."

Chapter Fourteen

CONSIDERING THE BODY IN TRAUMA

ONE OF THE REASONS I'm so passionate about listening to and supporting the body is the problem of trauma when dealing with grief.

Even when a death is expected, as was Stephen's, getting the bad news of a terminal diagnosis can be very traumatic. And the moment when your loved one actually leaves is equally stunning in its finality.

There is simply no way to comprehend the complete stillness that permeates a dead body. As long as Stephen was breathing, he was still here. But when his spirit took flight, he was so utterly gone that I could hardly catch my own breath.

And in the days and weeks immediately following his departure, what I dealt with most acutely was the feeling that my own heart had been amputated. Stephen didn't just take off alone, he took part of me with him.

The sensation was physical and agonizingly painful. It was also traumatic. This means that the emotional shock registered in the deepest recesses of my being—in those primal places where the natural response is to run from what feels like an attack, stand to fight it, or freeze in numbness from the overwhelming immensity of the experience.

This trauma reaction is so immediate that we don't even realize it has happened. There is so much to do when a person dies. I know I functioned on adrenalin for several days before collapsing in a dumb heap of sorrow.

And I did what a lot of people do—I processed my grief through physical movement. I was unconsciously trying to unlock that frozen trauma energy that gets stuck in our bodies until we allow the somatic aspects of grief and possibly even body-centered therapies to help us discharge the energy.

It was nearly two years before I happened to read Peter A. Levine's book, *Waking the Tiger: Healing Trauma* (North Atlantic Books, 1997). He describes how animals in the wild are naturally programmed to shake off the aborted fight-flight-freeze energy.

And he shows how we humans—with our sophisticated thinking brains—manage to subvert the process. We may decide, *we're just fine*, when we are actually exhibiting subtle symptoms of post-traumatic stress disorder (PTSD).

Much of the depression, nightmares, panic attacks, uncontrolled weeping, obsessions, sleep disturbances, and eating problems that we see in PTSD are often also presented by those who are grieving. So, which is it? PTSD or grief?

In my case, it was both. And I suspect that it is for many people. Because loss is not compartmentalized, it's cumulative. Loss compounds loss, especially if we don't process each one as it happens.

When childhood innocence is stolen by illness, abuse, or death, it is difficult for us to process those types of events. So when we are adults, perhaps experiencing the worst loss of our life in the death of a spouse or other loved one, time collapses and we're back in the thick of the original trauma.

For me, the original trauma was my sense that I was being killed when given ether anesthesia prior to a tonsillectomy at age three. I had known for many years that this was a pivotal experience in my childhood, but I did not know that it was considered a common source of PTSD in children of the 1950s until I read about it in Levine's book.

Simply reading that he considered this a clinically proven source of trauma gave me almost instant permission to time travel back into the experience. I was riding my stationary bicycle while reading, which probably help jump-start my reaction. Suddenly, in my mind's eye, I was yelling at the doctor, fighting back, getting away, liberating myself, and feeling the discharge of energy that had been stuck in me for fifty-six years.

The feelings produced a really dramatic crying jag. Fortunately, I was where I could be undisturbed, so I just went with it, wildly pedaling the whole time.

Psychodrama therapists know that nobody can stay in this kind of extremis for long. The body simply can't sustain it. So after about ten minutes, the crying stopped and I went to lie down. I was exhausted, but this time I wasn't frozen or numb. There was an aliveness to me, an invigoration that has remained.

This feeling of somatic freedom has also facilitated my continued grief journey. It is as if allowing myself to go so deep into my own primal recesses allowed me to contact a source of life and love that has resolved much of my sense of loss.

It is also easier for me to identify what loss I may

be mourning right now, rather than feeling that any loss triggers the sorrow of that original loss. I have been wounded, but I am no longer a walking wound. I am an individual who has had dramatic experiences that inform my being but that do not define me.

Being free from trauma, then, is a key to healing grief and continuing the journey of making contact with the most spiritual parts of self. And, from my experience, when we can do that, our journey increasingly becomes a walk with our spirit friends and loved ones who are just a breath away—if we will allow ourselves to be that free.

Chapter Fifteen

DEALING WITH
SUDDEN LOSS

FOR SOME TIME NOW, I have wanted to explore the subject of sudden loss because it can be an entirely different experience from dealing with a long illness, such as cancer.

In addition to several dear friends who have experienced a sudden loss, I have met people at book signings and workshops who have lost loved ones to accident, heart attack, suicide—even murder. In some ways, such experiences seem more difficult than loss that's drawn out over time, and I want to honor that difficulty here.

Having two and a half years after his terminal diagnosis to come to terms with Stephen's inevitable passing was a blessing for both of us. First of all, we were able to say "good-bye" and "thank you for loving me." We had time to put our financial affairs in order. Especially in his final year, we had many opportunities to commune together in the spirit of where we felt he was going. Our faith deepened, as did our love and sense of resolution with our individual challenges.

My friends whose loved ones died suddenly didn't get any of that. For many people, the traumatic shock of sudden loss can leave them stuck in that place of raw disbelief for years. At a recent book-signing event, I met a woman who had lost her husband to suicide ten years ago. She was so emotional that, when she started telling her story, I thought he must have died very recently. She had tried talk therapy to resolve her anger, despair, and hurt—but to no avail.

A dear friend of mine, whose husband died of a sudden heart attack, needed a couple of years to wrap her head around the fact that he wasn't coming back before she could get on with cleaning out his office. Another friend remains uncertain of how to dispose of her ex-husband's many collections because he didn't leave instruction about what was or was not important to him.

So, my sense is that there are two areas of sudden loss in which we need to be particularly sensitive. First is the seeming senselessness of the event. Despite our being emotional creatures, we humans are also innately rational. We want to know *why* something happened, what caused it, and what it means—especially in relation to ourselves.

And second, we must address the deep trauma that accompanies sudden loss. When we are hit with information that is too terrible to conceive, it is as if we have been physically struck.

Our body tenses. We recoil from the blow. Our breathing gets shallow. We become hyper-vigilant, waiting for the proverbial "next shoe" to drop. And if we are not able to resolve the fight-or-flight response of which these physical reactions are a part, we may become walking time capsules, stuck forever in that singular, tragic moment when our world fell apart.

I find myself returning to the key point that sudden loss is traumatic and, therefore, needs to be treated with even more sensitivity than anticipated loss. Of course, the loss of a loved one is always a shock—even when you know it's coming. But the shock of sudden loss gets even more profoundly lodged in the body as an aborted, physical reaction that must be healed through some kind of bodywork.

Talk therapy may help to eventually create meaning from the loss, but working with an experienced trauma therapist who is trained in somatic techniques such as EMDR or EFT is probably the first step in resolving the trauma.

Even in my situation, I know that allowing my body to release the trapped fight-or-flight energy made all the difference in my ability to once again embrace life .

Chapter Sixteen

WHY FAITH IS NOT ENOUGH

YESTERDAY A COLLEAGUE told me about a client whose husband had recently been diagnosed with early stage Alzheimer's. She was troubled about her ability to pay for the care that would likely consume their financial assets, and she was worried about being the kind of caregiver she wants to be.

"I feel so guilty," she told my colleague. "I've always tried to do the right thing and now this happens. I feel like I've done something wrong. Why else would this happen to us?"

What grieved me to hear this story is that the woman is a minister. Over the years she has helped countless people through life's burdens and now, in her own moment of crisis, she is also in a crisis of faith.

The more I read and talk to other death and grief educators, the more frequently I hear about religious people who find themselves in a similar state. In their anguish they cry out, *How could a loving God allow this to happen? This is so unfair. Why me?*

In a desperate attempt to find meaning in the unfathomable, they get stuck revolving their story of helplessness, hopelessness, sense of injustice, guilt, and victimhood. *This should not have happened*, they say to themselves, *and I cannot go on in the face of senseless tragedy.*

Why does this calamity of faith befall so many people—even clergy who have helped others in times of doubt? And what is the remedy?

I think one problem is that when tragedy strikes, it plunges us into a primal state in which survival and safety needs become the driving motivators. When we lose someone very dear, a part of us dies. Humans attach to things and people, and when the tie is broken, the part of us that lived in the other disappears. We may feel that we are dying—or that we would like to die. Without the presence of that person or thing, we feel abandoned, bereft, and vulnerable in a heartless world.

Faith does not necessarily address us in this desperately isolated place. In this kind of loss, we are operating in a physical/emotional state while faith is a more cerebral function that operates in the realm of ideas—even if those ideas are passionately believed.

We may strongly adhere to a tenet of an immortal soul, a loving Universe, or a just God. But until we have empirical evidence of the truth of these precepts, our faith remains theoretical, abstract. And—judging from the number of people I've witnessed whose faith appears to fail them—simple faith is not enough when change is powerfully negative.

So, how are we to find meaning and solace in the face of what may be the worst thing that ever happened to us? I'd like to suggest that we find it in a way that bridges the gap between ideas and stories—in the realm of regular practice.

What do I mean by practice? For many of us, practice is an activity that results in a tangible feeling of physical empowerment, mental and emotional calm, and a sense of being connected with our true self—even with something higher or deeper than that self.

There is a "now" aspect to practice that releases tension in the body and eases away our frantic thoughts. Yoga and meditation have long been such practices. Walking, running, swimming, martial arts such as tai chi, or music, painting, dancing, and writing can all produce the same effect. Mindfulness and the Tibetan compassion meditation called *tonglen* also work.

What we are looking for is any regularly practiced activity that puts us deeply in touch with the present moment. Because in that place of simple being, doctrine and dogma become irrelevant. The only thing that matters is the connection that says, *In this place, I know who I am and I am grounded in that being.*

That knowing is the rock of our stability. And in times of crisis, it becomes the life raft we ride to a shore of safety and equilibrium. It is also the place in which meaning eventually finds us.

Having a practice of stillness anchors us in a state of awareness where we can remain grounded in what is happening now, rather than spinning off into suppositions of *What if?* or *If only.* In moments of crisis, it teaches detachment from strong emotions.

This is not to say that we become unfeeling zombies who stumble mindlessly through life untouched by the suffering of others. On the contrary. If anything, it allows us to more acutely experience the moment— whether it be happy or sad—and to return to baseline more quickly.

If we have a momentum on connecting with self, when life goes awry, we don't question who or what we are. We know that our identity is not dependent on precepts or traditions because we have experienced self in the simplicity of its "is-ness." And we know that our identity will survive dramatic change because it has already survived previous episodes of upheaval.

Practice becomes a valuable tool for profound self-exploration. Being aware of that energy in the body can be helpful—especially when change propels us into new circumstances or very deep emotions such as anger.

For example, I have seen skilled facilitators bring distraught people into equilibrium and powerful insight by following the physical sensation of a powerful emotion to its source. Even thoughts of suicide after losing a beloved child can provide meaning when allowed to speak for themselves in the loving presence of a facilitator who trusts the dynamic of personal process.

So, having some kind of daily centering practice becomes a psychological insurance policy against the day when life throws us a curve ball. Because practice creates a physical sense of safety and an experience of the survivability of self, when we lose our outer moorings, our inner ones remain intact.

Our faith may be tested by difficult circumstances, but it is less likely to be shattered if we are practiced in being present with the self that lives independent of belief systems. Faith may be challenged by hardship, but through the experience of spiritual presence it may also deepen into a new resiliency of soul that sustains and strengthens us—even allowing us to help others along the way.

Chapter Seventeen

THE POWER OF
STORY TO HEAL

WHEN I HEAR THE PHRASE, "Once upon a time," my ears perk up, my heart opens, and I feel my body relax in anticipation of something magical. It's automatic and it happens every time. And if a story is not actually forth-coming, I make up one in my head.

I seem to be wired for story, and my experience and research tell me that other people are too. Humans are natural storytellers. It is our most innate form of verbal communication.

Since the beginning of human history, when some-thing happens that we want to share with others, we tell them a story. For centuries we have told tales sitting around campfires or walking on pilgrimage to holy sites. With the advent of mechanical transport, we began sharing our experiences aboard ship, on trains, planes, and prairie schooners.

And at the end of our life, if we were fortunate, we were graced with a kind listener who would witness the story of our days on earth as only we could tell it.

From infancy we are schooled in the essence of story. It must have a beginning, a middle, and an end. A good one immediately draws us in with some version of "long ago and far away." The middle is full of action, drama, conflict, suspense. There is a moral dilemma, a problem to solve, a villain to thwart, a rescue to effect. Often the hero must make a choice—the consequences of which determine how the story will end.

And in the end, we expect resolution. The good guys win. Evil is vanquished and love prevails. The villagers are once again snug in their beds, and all is right with the world. We breathe a sigh of relief as the minor chords of conflict resolve to major and the last flourish sounds in triumph.

But life is not so tidy—its conundrums not so easily resolved. Bad things happen to nice people, and the good guys don't always win. This can throw us into a state of confusion, even a crisis of faith—the result being a sense of perpetual sadness from which we feel power-less to escape.

In this state, our affinity for story can turn either destructive or liberating. It all depends on the flavor of the tale we tell. For example, negative story is power-fully wounding:

I should have known something was wrong.

Why didn't he ask for help?

She never really loved me.

They were so young.

How could a just God let this happen?

You were always irresponsible.

This tragedy has ruined my life.

Each time a negative story is repeated, it winds another coil of bitterness, disappointment, anger, resentment, sorrow, guilt, desperation—even hatred—until the teller is bound up in a shroud of darkness that becomes a prison to the mind and heart.

In this black place, the light of healing does not shine—unless we can change the flavor of the story. Because a positive story acts like a spiritual Balm of Gilead, it heals the deepest wounds of head and heart, setting us on a path to fresh meaning and a bright new tomorrow.

I discovered this phenomenon almost immediately after my husband's death. If I spent too much time alone in my thoughts, in the house that still echoed from Stephen's departure, my story was desperately sad. But as soon as I talked to other people, telling them about his graceful passing, his unique perspective on life, or the spiritual insights he had shared with me, the stories were uplifting—to me as well as to my listeners.

What astonished me in these early days was a relentless need to tell my story to anybody who would listen. I wanted to talk and talk. And there were certain events I felt compelled to relate over and over, as if each repetition was a key to unlocking a hidden treasure I could not articulate, but whose presence I could feel.

I now believe that treasure was meaning—a way to make sense of my experience so I could move on from it. Until I could say with some certainty that I understood why Stephen had died and why I was still here, living without him was nearly unbearable.

Chapter Eighteen

THE NARRATIVE
OF LOVE AND SOUL

BECAUSE STEPHEN HAD CANCER—which gave us time to discuss these things—we found deep meaning in our mutual conviction of the soul's desire for union with the Divine.

In sharing Saint-Exupéry's beloved tale, *The Little Prince*, we realized how we had tamed each other—Stephen calmed me down and I opened him up. And before that, I had had a vision that our ongoing mission was to inspire others to approach the end of life with love and intention.

But those were shared meanings. What I sought after he died was new logic for my solo life that could conceivably last many, many years. If I was to remain alone, I needed to know why.

I found multiple reasons in the process of telling our story. I wrote a book to capture Stephen's legacy of love and service. I wrote it to convince myself that our lives had been profoundly guided and that I could continue to live in the palm of God's hand.

I wrote the book to comfort others facing similar circumstances. And in the process of writing, I gained fresh insight into the heart of this remarkable man.

There were times when I got stuck. My editor asked for more setup to certain events. She wanted to know what we were thinking and feeling, not just what happened. I could reconstruct my own mental and emotional state, but Stephen's was a mystery—until he would send it to me in a dream or moment of intuitive inspiration.

It was as if he were telling me another part of his story from beyond the veil so that I could understand him better. In my heart of hearts, I believe our loved ones can do this for us—even if we forget to ask them. And the vehicle they often use is story.

I believe that storytelling is a faculty of the soul. In personal narrative, we ease into that mystical space between worlds where a more universal view is possible and merciful insight flows like water. In this place, it is as though the Master Storyteller is letting us in on life's secrets, pulling back the curtain to reveal forces at work behind the scenes.

Suddenly we see causes behind effects that had heretofore been our only experience on the stage of life. Now we get it:

So-and-so wasn't evil; he was misguided.

Losing that job liberated me to find a better one.

I had learned all I could from that marriage.

The other person forgave me long ago.

In other words, those bad things happened to good people—not because God is cynical or cruel—

but because sometimes things just happen here in the imperfect world of time and space.

We may have to create our own silver lining, but the process puts us closer to the ever-present divinity within. If we keep digging deeper into underlying causes, I believe we can ultimately discover that the soul's desire for deep spiritual connection flows through all of our human experience.

Even in cases of abject evil, we may realize—as Nazi death camp survivor Victor Frankl has powerfully demonstrated—that the human soul's search for meaning can prevail in the most horrendous of circumstances.

How we embody that essential motivation is really the greatest story ever told. And locking into that narrative of love and soul is what gives story its astonishing power to heal.

Chapter Nineteen

HONORING THE
CIRCLE OF GRIEF

I WROTE THE ARTICLE BELOW a couple of weeks before
a dear friend died. I had known for months that he was
terminally ill, but most of our mutual friends didn't—
he had sworn me to secrecy. So, when I felt his situation
pressing on my awareness, all I could do was pour my
heart out on the page, speaking to the Universe in hopes
that my message might reach him.

One aspect of palliative care and hospice that I most
appreciate is the attention to the community of concern
that surrounds the person who is ill or dying. Not only
is the whole patient supported—mentally, emotionally,

physically, and spiritually—so is the family. Because when one person suffers, many hearts feel the pain.

Of course, we think of spouses, siblings, parents, children—all those with family ties to the patient. But we often forget about friends who, after decades of shared experiences at work and in community, may actually be emotionally closer than some relatives.

It's a tricky balance to include everyone who is concerned, especially when someone is terminally ill. When we first learned that Stephen's cancer was incurable, we wanted to just crawl into a cave and disappear. Having to convey such terrible news to our loved ones and deal with their emotions as well as our own felt absolutely overwhelming.

Stephen never did confide in more than a handful of people at his workplace, but I knew we needed prayer support. So, I kept up an e-mail correspondence with a dozen or so close friends. I know their prayers made a difference to us.

One Sunday morning Stephen and I paused in our devotional reading because we could feel our own burdens being lifted by the hearts of our friends. And that support has continued to make all the difference to me in my journey without my beloved.

Recently, several of these friends expressed their appreciation for being included in our journey— something that had never occurred to me. In fact, only now do I fully comprehend that Stephen's family and I are not the only ones who grieve his loss.

Stephen was a very private person who did not open himself to many people, but those who knew him cherished the connection. And when he died, they wept over their own loss of a true and noble friend. I knew we needed our friends, but now I see that they also needed to be needed.

The physical pain of a terminal illness can be very isolating. Dealing with the body's demise rivets your attention, making it difficult to reach out. Especially if you are the patient or the caregiver, it is natural for your peripheral vision to become increasingly narrow. But I think those in the wider circle of friendship fare better if we can acknowledge their concern and enlist their loving support.

I am struck by how connected I feel with a wide circle of friends. Many of us had lived and worked together for twenty years or more. These days we are scattered around the world, but we are being drawn closer by the losses that seem to be piling up around us.

My oldest childhood friend lost her husband to cancer a few weeks ago. My sister-in-law lost her brother suddenly last month. An acquaintance died after a long battle with breast cancer.

I have at least three close friends who are dealing with advanced illnesses. Three others are facing difficult challenges with chronically ill elderly parents. And a colleague just learned that his buddy has metastatic colon cancer.

So, we are—all of us—surrounded with loss and grief. We are in this together. Yet, when we're in the battle ourselves, it's hard not to feel alone. And it's tempting to be more alone than may be necessary.

I think there are a couple of reasons for this. First of all, we may not be geographically close to those to whom we feel most emotionally tied.

Secondly, if we've been highly competent, the sudden sense of vulnerability from a terminal diagnosis can shatter our confidence and self-esteem. I am quite sure that feeling his mind and body wasting away was one of Stephen's greatest trials because he had always been so mentally and physically strong.

I also think there is an element of shame and self-criticism that the patient has to deal with—particularly in the case of spiritual seekers who may have a strong belief in the power of mind over matter.

The idea that we can create our own illnesses or cures may have some validity, but it may also be an unnecessary burden to one who is ill. I've had cancer survivors tell me, "Oh, I got over that mindset a long time ago. I had to, or I couldn't have gone on."

Ultimately, we don't know why some people get sick and recover while others get sick and die. If we did, we would certainly do a better job of preventing what seem to be untimely deaths.

But that's not how it works. Life happens. It's not all happy endings. We live in an increasingly toxic environment and we are vulnerable in ways our ancestors never imagined. We have better medical technology, but we also seem to have more virulent diseases. And my Baby Boomer friends and I are getting older, which means that we are losing one another.

As I tune in to the hearts of those who are facing great physical challenges and those who are grieving a loss that may have come all too soon, my concern is that we honor our connections even as we honor the need for sensitivity to each one's way of coping.

Sooner or later we must each find our own way through the valley of the shadow of death. I have done a lot of grieving alone and am grateful for the solitude that allows me to plumb the very depths of loss without fear of embarrassment or intrusion upon other people.

But I have also done some of my most profound healing in the company of those who have loved me and held a space of unconditional acceptance and safety where both grief and resolution could unfold.

So, may we pray for one another. May we remember to ask for prayers from those who would be only too happy to send us spiritual support.

May we be kind in thinking of our friends. Grateful for heart ties that still bind us together over miles and years. And may we remember that when one of us suffers or dies, we all feel the pain and the loss.

Accepting that fact connects us in ways more profound than we can imagine. And that, to me, is cause for hope—even when it hurts.

Chapter Twenty

TIME TRAVELING
THROUGH LOSS

ONE THING I HAVE LEARNED in the past couple of years is that we do not grieve just once. We move through loss and, with work and compassion toward self and others, we can move forward. What is fascinating to me is how we also move back in time when loss hits us again.

My friend Gwen clued me in to this phenomenon a few weeks ago when Sam, the husband of our mutual childhood friend, died of liver cancer. Here's how Gwen put it: "When my father died, my mother had already been gone for a couple of years. But losing him felt like I had also just lost her—it was that fresh. Now that Sam is gone, it's as if Stephen Eckl has died all over again."

This past weekend, I got a taste of exactly what Gwen was describing. I had flown to Montana to attend the memorial service of another dear friend, colleague, and spiritual brother. It was a poignant event that included the reunion of many friends who hadn't seen each other in more than a decade.

I had already done a lot of processing with others by phone and e-mail. So, while deeply saddened by the loss of this wonderful person, I was doing okay—until I saw his photo on the program and the service began.

Suddenly, I was in a time warp—simultaneously in the church in Montana and a chapel in Colorado where Stephen's service had taken place in 2008. The grief was raw. Sobs welled up in my throat and my heart broke all over again. Two and a half years between events collapsed into a single moment.

Intellectually, I knew this was different. Although they were both very private Scorpio men, my friend was not Stephen. But grief didn't care. To grief, loss is loss.

Any loss relates to all losses. And dramatic loss means plunging into the depths of sorrow—regardless of the cause or the timetable. This is the way of grief that I have espoused, so I went with it.

Deep personal loss is so painful. It is astonishingly physical. And, like a severe bodily wound, it can take a long time to heal. It is natural to grit our teeth and just press on so we are not overcome with the immediate pain. I believe this is one reason why we need community to help us stay with and express our grief rather than denying or dissociating from it.

So, here is what I witnessed this weekend as over two hundred people joined in tribute to a great man's life:

- Open, authentic, and mutual sadness from all those who had loved our friend
- Compassion for one another as well as for his family
- Joy that so many longtime friends had come together for this event

- Celebration of the spirit of community that was once again kindled
- Genuine appreciation of how we have touched one another's lives
- And heartfelt gratitude for the work that had originally brought us all together so many years ago.

———————————

As we celebrated the life of our friend and spiritual brother, we wept—not only for our loss, but also in recognition of our unity. In those precious hours of communion, I believe many experienced a compression of previous losses into this single one. But because we were together, it was easier to also feel the timeless bond of brotherhood that, once forged, is truly eternal.

Sadness turned into a poignant joy. This was a love-fest with more hugs than I have ever experienced in one place. We cried hard. But, by the end of the day, we were laughing much harder. And as we made our way home, many of us felt that our friend's memorial service was actually his greatest service of all—because it allowed us to follow the process of grief all the way through to collective transformation.

So, now I understand another facet of grief's wisdom. The ability of any loss to compress time into an experience of all loss means we must be mindful of processing each loss as it comes—lest it compound into a pain too difficult to bear.

But this phenomenon also means that the possibility of ever-deeper healing is always present. And the more trustingly we follow the wisdom of grief, the more surely we will experience the comfort that awaits those who truly mourn.

Chapter Twenty-One

MOTHER NATURE REMINDS ME TO LIVE

AFTER SEVERAL WEEKS of relentless computer work, my body was begging me to go outside today and soak up some delicious March sunshine. Having little motivation to do much else, I put on a pair of gardening gloves, got out the clippers and rake, and went to work on some dead foliage that needed a pre-spring haircut.

How delightful to discover that, under the dried leaves and brown grasses, new shoots are already sprouting. I even have a tulip pushing up through the soil in a warm, sheltered place against the house.

These little slips of green may be laughable to people like my cousin in Atlanta who already has daffodils and redbud in bloom. But here in Colorado—where it's really not safe to plant much of anything until at least the middle of May—seeing life in the flowerbeds in early March is a delightful surprise.

Digging in the dirt felt so good. It is no accident that we talk about "grounding." And yet, how easily we forget about nature and the life force that emanates from the earth. Focusing on weeding and snipping cleared my mind and gave it something else to chew on—such as the metaphor of how life periodically prunes the dross from our consciousness so the green shoots of healing can emerge.

Nature is available to support me if I'll just pay attention and get outside. This becomes increasingly important because Stephen isn't here to ground me with his physical presence—one of the reasons I miss him so desperately.

My feeling has long been that he was able to reach very high spiritually because he was very grounded in the earth. He was so anchored in reality and practicality that I have described him as walking on four legs. He was working on a heavy equipment crew when I fell in love with him, and I think that may have been his all-time favorite job.

Stephen was just crazy about moving dirt! And as I continue to discover aspects of his personality that I have absorbed and remember lessons that he taught me by simply being who and what he was, I can see that emulating his affection for the earthiness of earth could be a very good idea.

So, after spending countless hours writing about endings, I am reminded of how exuberantly Mother Nature is dedicated to beginnings. She never fails to bring forth new growth from even the deadest looking material.

Surely, I can do no less in my own life.

Chapter Twenty-Two

THE GIFT OF GRIEF

THE LATE CELTIC WISE MAN, poet, and philosopher John O'Donohue says that whatever is real in us can risk the fires of grief. That ultimately grief burns up only what is useless and false, and that it leaves behind a gift of purity and insight and a heart newly tender, open, and deeply attuned to the transcendent.

He is probably right, but it didn't feel that way when I was walking through the fires of my own intense sorrow. The heat was all consuming when I was in it. And whatever was being torched complained bitterly.

Not always, of course. During the daytime I was mostly okay. I could imagine that Stephen was merely at work while I was busy writing. I was finding meaning in that work and, as long as I was in the story, Stephen felt very present.

But when he didn't come home at dinnertime—again!—the darkness set in. The emptiness enveloped me like a cloak, and the blank place where my amputated heart used to be filled up with tears that flooded out in a torrent of sorrow. They came from a place so deep that I felt it would swallow me whole. Or that I would sink so low that hope and life would never find me again.

For months I just couldn't think of any good reason to keep on living. I did, of course. We who mourn may feel like we're dying of grief, but few of us actually do. As much as grief seems fatal, it isn't—at least not to what in us is authentically durable. And therein lies the mystery.

In some ways, I've come through the worst part—at least I hope so. Grief is a dynamic process and, for me, the deepest agony seems to be past. Either that, or I've become more careful about not putting myself into circumstances that trigger a crying jag. The former, if true, is a comfort. The potential of the latter concerns me—lest I push to heal too quickly and miss the grace of allowing grief to do its secret work in me for as long as it will.

Because I do consider it a grace to grieve. Not to wallow in self-pity and perpetual sorrow, but to follow the stream of wise grief as it washes away false notions of human control and replaces them with the power of vulnerability and a heart that knows compassion for the suffering of others.

That is the gift of grief I don't want to lose.

Chapter Twenty-Three

THE COMFORT THAT
IS ALREADY THERE

THERE IS A LOW, soulful tone in the word "mourn"—a word whose sounding replicates the feeling of actually being in that state. To mourn is to enter into the deepest region of human feeling, into that primal place of our greatest vulnerability and, surprisingly, our greatest strength.

The idea of mourning carries an image of sackcloth and ashes—of publicly weeping and wailing and rending one's garments. Of so surrendering to the severity of loss that our knees buckle under the weight of despair.

I must confess that years ago, when I observed scenes of what I viewed as overwrought emotionalism portrayed on the news from far-away places, I considered them decidedly un-modern. I would hold myself aloof from such histrionics and vow that my own grief—should it come—would never devolve into this kind of narcissistic drama. (Little did I know what life had in store for me.)

Our Western culture believes that expressions of loss are meant to be brief, tidy, dignified, and not intrusive on other people. The problem is that confining our sorrow to such a neatly bordered experience also makes it ineffective. We may remain in control, but we do not find comfort, and we do not heal.

In his seminal work, *When Bad Things Happen to Good People* (Anchor Books, 1981), Rabbi Harold S. Kushner comes to the conclusion that God is not in control of what happens to us in our lives, but that the Divine is always present. The key is tapping into that Presence to find the comfort promised by faith traditions the world around.

Kushner suggests that one way is to change the question of suffering from, *Why me?* to *What shall I do now that calamity has visited my life?* For Stephen and me, the question became, *Why not us?* and *How can we turn this experience into something meaningful?*

Throughout his illness, we continually asked ourselves, *To whom can we turn for help?* And the answer was always, *To God.*

The matter of random and deliberate evil looms large when dealing with why bad things happen to good people. Kushner's own preference for order and predictability is evident in the way he labels chaos as evil and creation as making order out of chaos.

But for new creation to emerge, the old order must be disturbed—sometimes dramatically. And if this is true, then chaos and creation are neither evil nor righteous. Instead, they can be seen as engaged in a dance of yin and yang, feminine and masculine, dark and light, moon and sun, negative and positive polarities.

These forces of nature are neither moral nor discriminating. They simply are. What matters is how we respond to them in the flow of our lives—which leads us to the subject of pain and suffering, especially as we grieve and mourn the emptiness that even mild loss leaves in its wake.

Kushner says that pain is "nature's way of warning . . . that something is wrong"—perhaps that we are overexerting ourselves. In the case of loss, it tells us that something important is missing. Where once there was order, now chaos has erupted. A beloved pattern has been displaced. And, if we are to thrive, the old must be creatively replaced by the new.

If God is the source of this creative help, how do we access it? Where do we go when life feels hopeless and there are no answers—only a silent room or an empty chair at the table where our loved one used to sit?

From the early days of my own grief, experience has shown that true and lasting comfort arises when I allow myself to ease from the relative superficiality of sadness into a primal place of uncontrollable tears where my heart breaks open—all the way down into abject mourning where I experience the uselessness of human pride and intellect.

In that dark place, I lay myself upon the altar of God's wise mercy. And in that act of surrender to what is happening, divine support and comfort flood into my soul as a fresh summer rain on parched soil.

Except for clinging to a desire for control and predictability, I wonder if perhaps I could have tapped into this soul relief sooner. But I am reminded that Stephen once said we often need dramatic loss to push us to the limits of mental reasoning where love and comfort abide. So what deep mourning opens is access to the flow of unconditional love that is always available—even before calamity strikes.

You can tell when people have truly mourned because of how they greet life's challenges. Rather than resisting the chaos of old patterns crumbling, they embrace the potential creativity of new ones emerging—which is not to say that they no longer feel pain. In fact, they may feel it more acutely than others who have not walked this path.

But rather than hovering in a no-man's land of depression or regret, they go willingly into the dark in confidence that there are always layers of grasping to surrender and new levels of love and comfort to be experienced.

God may not be in charge of daily events, but my experience tells me that Spirit has answered our cry for help even before we utter it. We are wired to feel pain, to have our hearts broken, and to mourn profoundly. And when we do, the Divine is always already there.

Chapter Twenty-Four

THE ART OF
LETTING GO

TODAY IS THE THIRD ANNIVERSARY of my husband's death from colon cancer. I honestly cannot say what that means. I can only observe that I am changing or possibly that he is changing or perhaps both.

At any rate, my experience of life is not what it was. Nor is my experience of grief. It tastes different—as if my salty tears have lost some of their savor.

Grief also feels different. Somehow it is more spacious these days and, oddly, more full. I cry less from the sorrow of Stephen's absence and more joyfully from the poignant presence of my authentic Self that has filled in so much of the heart space he once occupied.

For the past year I have been aware of a lot of movement going on between us as we work out our separate
lives on opposite sides of the veil between this world and
the next. I am astonished at how much I have accom-
plished and I sense that Stephen has been busy, too.

Several months ago I noticed that he seemed to
be hanging out about a block away, just over the street,
waving at me that he was still around, but not nearly as
close as when I was writing our story.

In recent weeks I have had the impression that
he was frequently away and at an even greater remove.
I knew I could call on him if necessary, but it seemed
selfish and self-indulgent to do so.

When I thought about it, I realized that I was
healing—becoming stronger at all levels of being. I
was becoming less dependent on my connection with
Stephen and more confident in my ability to move
forward without him.

That doesn't mean I have not grieved anew over the

stark feeling that a cycle has ended. It is as if I am once more being eased out of a cosmic nest. Unbeknownst to me, I've been growing a new set of wings that are more powerful, more resilient, more confident.

How funny. I thought I was trying to become a better writer and get others to notice how hard I've been working. But this week it has become clear— Stephen and I have different obligations right now.

I feel certain we will always remain joined at the heart and that, should I really need him, he will come to my aid. But I don't need him that way at the moment, and he doesn't need me as he once did.

We have come to another fork in the road. Oh, how hard it is to write those words. But it's true—I'm letting go again. Not by consciously releasing anything, but simply by observing that Stephen is letting go of me, naturally slipping away into other realms of being.

One of my great worries in losing Stephen's physical presence was that I would come unhinged without him. He was like the grounding wire in my electrical circuit. All I had to do was plug in with him and then I would be back in the flow.

But I do remember that feeling of connection, and it seems that I have internalized enough of my own inner grounding that he feels confident in leaving me to go on with his other work. Or, perhaps, it is simply what must be in the universal scheme of things.

I have moved my photos of him to places of less prominence, replacing them with images that support the creative direction that's calling me. The snapshots of us hiking, hugging, laughing, and joking are still meaningful, but I cannot cling to what is now so obviously in the past.

This is another level of my human brain realizing, *Oh, he really is gone, isn't he?* The great cosmic *duh!* that seems so hard to admit, even after three years.

As I allow myself to sit with the changes that are happening, Stephen now appears as a glimmer in a distant solar system, a unique star in the firmament of my awareness. Last night I recalled that a couple of days before he died I sang to him, "I'll be looking at the stars, and I'll be seeing you."

He was delighted that I would make such a promise. And I'm glad I did because it's truer now than I ever suspected it might be.

Coda

SINGING WHILE
IT IS STILL DARK

IN ONE OF MY favorite verses by David Whyte, this beloved poet of the inner life writes:

> anything or anyone
> that does not bring you alive
>
> is too small for you.
>
> ("Sweet Darkness")

Could it be that grief has become too small for me? That's what it feels like—which is astonishing, really, because for at least three years it has felt much too large.

The sheer, random power of grief has overwhelmed me, sometimes for days or weeks at a time, rendering me unable to move with any sort of clarity or purpose other than trying hard not to expire on the spot.

But things are different now. I do not dread the occasional rush of tears that flood out of nowhere. In fact, I almost welcome them as a sign that I have encountered a deep truth about the inner workings of my heart, mind, and soul. Eyes welling up has become a sure response to beauty, and a catch in my throat means that I am receptive to the poignancy of life itself.

These are all good omens that point to a new life dawning out of loss. I am grateful to see them because I am not by nature a sad person. While I have tried not to rush through grief's ineluctable process, I am very happy to recognize a bit of the old me resurfacing.

Of course, I will never again be the "old me." How could I? The tapestry of my being will forever contain the golden threads of my late husband's love, woven through with grey threads of death and the dark crimson threads of heartbreak.

But it is not a tight weave. There are holes where rays of yellow sunshine break through and the warm breeze of hope wafts in, calling me to a new life that is just beginning to glisten with creative possibility.

But what is that life? I feel its call into a cycle of change, but the direction is unclear. Of course, I remind myself. That's the way it is at the threshold. Whenever we enter a new frontier, all the old familiarities pass away. Even the grieving process can become a security blanket once we are accustomed to the way it works in us. And for me, that's a warning.

Life has never let me get too comfortable. So it's really no surprise that just about the time I would realize a certain facility with the language of grief and loss, a new wave of thought and feeling should start knocking at the door of my heart, urging me to entertain a fresh adventure.

However, even that invitation sparks a certain caution. Despite my love of beginnings, I have also learned to appreciate endings. And the best lesson is that we don't get out of anything unless we love our way through to its natural conclusion.

With an experience as painful as grief, it is all too tempting to flee at the first sign of relief. But that's not the way it works. There is always a transition time in which we must cohabitate with both the old that is ending and the new that has not quite emerged.

Elsewhere David Whyte says:

> What you can plan
> is too small
> for you to live.
> ("What to Remember When Waking")

Drat! I'm sure he means that any future I can conceive of right now will pale before what actually unfolds in its own sweet time. So, patience and more patience—and the familiar requirement of self-observation and attention to what remains undone in the current cycle of death and rebirth.

Gestation of anything worth living takes the time that nature prescribes, not me. Much as I would like, I cannot force the bud of new experience, especially when there still is work to do.

In some ways, I feel like I have written to the very bottom of my own barrel of grief. That may be true, but I haven't written to the bottom of other people's thought or experience. And other experts have much to say that I am now free to explore and incorporate into my work.

So, I am comforted by an old Scandinavian saying I ran across this past week: "Faith is a bird that feels the dawn breaking and sings while it is still dark."

The future has not yet dawned, but I'm singing away—even as I keep my ears open for the new melody.

I know it's coming soon.

ACKNOWLEDGMENTS

Writing a Collection of thoughts and musings alone in my room and then turning them into a book is a bit like the difference between singing solo or singing in a choir. When other hearts and voices join in, the sound is richer, deeper, more profound, and ultimately more capable of uplifting both listeners and singers.

A Beautiful Grief is one such heartwarming collaboration with people I have known for years and with others only recently met in bookstores, on phone calls, in workshops, and through amazing conversations shared online.

My walk with grief has been incredibly blessed as I continue to grow through the outlet of writing, first in my own blog and then as one of many contributors on the *Psychology Today* website—an opportunity for which I am truly grateful.

The articles and conversations that emerged from these blogs settled themselves into this collection of musings that I have imagined as a bedside companion— a voice of compassionate understanding from someone who has been where you are or where you may be going, and who knows you can make it to a new tomorrow.

Many thanks go to my colleagues: Anne Barthel, James Bennett, and Theresa McNicholas. And to count-less readers, clients, colleagues, and unseen helpers who have inspired me with your questions, comments, and insights.

Thank you all for helping to guide me forward on a journey that is increasingly beautiful, even as grief has played out its wistful melody from sorrow to resolution and joy.

CHERYL LAFFERTY ECKL is an award-winning author, mystical poet, and storyteller. Since the death of her husband, she has developed an abundance of material focused on transforming loss into renewal and self-transcendence. She holds a master's certificate in Transpersonal Psychology and is passionate about helping others navigate the rough waters of loss.

Cheryl lives in Montana, where the rarefied atmosphere of Big Sky country inspires her to pay deep attention to the music of what's happening—to learn and grow, and then share those insights with others. She is the author of multiple books.

Learn more at www.CherylEckl.com.

CPSIA information can be obtained
at www.ICGtesting.com
Printed in the USA
JSHW030902140722
28038JS00003B/178

9 780982 810729